P9-DDB-964

Nuclear Submarines

by Michael Burgan

Consultant:
Captain James Hay, USN (Ret.)
Editor, *The Submarine Review*
Naval Submarine League

CAPSTONE
HIGH-INTEREST
BOOKS

an imprint of Capstone Press
Mankato, Minnesota

Capstone High-Interest Books are published by Capstone Press
151 Good Counsel Drive, P.O. Box 669, Mankato, Minnesota 56002
http://www.capstone-press.com

Library of Congress Cataloging-in-Publication Data
Burgan, Michael.
    Nuclear submarines/by Michael Burgan.
    p. cm.—(Land and sea)
    Includes bibliographical references (p. 45) and index.
    ISBN 0-7368-0759-4
    1. Nuclear submarines—United States—Juvenile literature. [1. Nuclear
submarines. 2. Submarines.] I. Title. II. Land and sea (Mankato, Minn.)
V857.5 .B87 2001
359.9'3834'0973—dc21   00-009825

Summary: Describes the history, design, weapons, and missions of nuclear submarines.

Editorial Credits
Carrie A. Braulick, editor; James Franklin, cover designer; Timothy Halldin,
    production designer and illustrator; Katy Kudela, photo researcher

Photo Credits
Archive Photos, 10, 15; Earl Young/Archive Photos, 4
Defense Visual Information Center, cover
Photri-Microstock, 7, 8, 12, 17, 21, 22, 27, 28, 31, 32, 34, 36, 38, 41, 42
Reuters/Jim Bourg/Archive Photos, 18

1 2 3 4 5 6 06 05 04 03 02 01

Table of Contents

Chapter One

Nuclear Submarines

The U.S. Navy uses many kinds of warships. These ships carry guns, missiles, and other weapons. Submarines are warships that can travel on top of the water as other warships do. But submarines also can travel underwater. People often call submarines "subs."

The U.S. Navy's group of submarines sometimes is called the "Silent Service." These subs are designed to travel quietly underwater. Quiet ships are difficult for enemy forces to locate.

Nuclear Subs

The Navy commissioned its first sub in 1900. Subs that are in commission are in active

The Navy's nuclear submarines travel quietly underwater.

service. A gasoline engine powered this sub when it traveled on the surface. A battery powered the sub when it was submerged. Later subs used diesel-electric engines. These engines used diesel fuel when they traveled on the surface. Battery-operated motors powered the subs when they were submerged. Diesel-electric subs needed to rise to the surface to get air for their diesel engines. They also needed to refuel regularly.

In the mid 1950s, the Navy began to use nuclear-powered subs. Nuclear power forms when the metal uranium produces energy by splitting its atoms. Atoms are extremely small pieces of matter. A nuclear sub's fuel can last for more than 25 years. Nuclear subs do not need air for their engines as diesel-electric subs do. The subs can stay submerged for months at a time. Nuclear subs also travel faster and dive deeper than diesel-electric subs do. All of the U.S. Navy's subs now use

Fleet ballistic missile subs are part of the Navy's nuclear submarine force.

nuclear power. But some other countries still use diesel-electric subs.

Types of Nuclear Subs

The Navy has two basic types of nuclear subs. These types are attack subs and fleet ballistic missile subs. Attack subs are designed to carry out many different tasks in naval warfare. They often perform anti-submarine warfare (ASW).

They locate and destroy enemy subs. They also attack other types of enemy warships. In peacetime, they patrol the waters near possible conflict areas.

Attack subs use a variety of weapons to destroy enemy warships. They may fire torpedoes. These explosives travel underwater. Attack subs also can launch missiles at ships on the surface or at targets on land. The subs can launch the missiles while they are submerged. Attack subs also lay mines on the ocean floor.

Fleet ballistic missile subs carry large nuclear missiles. These subs sometimes are called "boomers." The Navy has never launched a nuclear missile at an enemy from a sub. It uses real missiles with dummy warheads to test the subs. Warheads are the explosive part of missiles.

Fleet ballistic missile submarines stay hidden in the oceans. Enemies usually cannot locate these subs. This feature helps prevent the enemies from starting wars. The missiles can be very harmful to enemies.

Attack subs may fire missiles at ships on the surface or at land targets.

Chapter Two

History

During the late 1930s, scientists learned how to produce nuclear energy. In the late 1940s, Hyman Rickover thought of using nuclear energy to power submarines. Rickover was a U.S. Navy captain. He formed a team to install a nuclear-powered engine on a sub. Some people call Rickover "the father of the nuclear Navy."

In 1954, the U.S. Navy commissioned the world's first nuclear submarine. This sub was called the *Nautilus*. The *Nautilus* could travel at 23 knots. One knot equals about 1.15 miles (1.85 kilometers) per hour. This speed was about 8 knots faster than diesel-electric subs could travel on the surface. The *Nautilus* also

Hyman Rickover helped design the first nuclear sub.

The Navy commissioned the *Nautilus* in 1954.

could travel submerged at its top speed for
many days. Diesel-electric subs could only
travel at top speed while submerged for about
30 minutes.

Fleet Ballistic Missile Subs
In 1959, the Navy commissioned its first
fleet ballistic missile sub. It was called the
George Washington. The sub was 380 feet

(116 meters) long and had a displacement of 6,700 tons (6,078 metric tons). Displacement is the weight of the water that would fill the space taken up by a sub. *George Washington* carried 16 nuclear missiles.

The Navy built four more subs with the same features as the original *George Washington*. These subs made up the *George Washington* class. All of the Navy's subs in a class have similar features. Each class is named for the first sub built in that class.

In the late 1960s, the Navy built new fleet ballistic missile subs. These subs were in the *Lafayette* and *Benjamin Franklin* classes. Subs in these classes could carry larger nuclear missiles than the *George Washington*-class subs.

In 1981, the Navy commissioned *Ohio*-class fleet ballistic missile subs. These are the only fleet ballistic missile subs the Navy uses today. *Ohio*-class subs are 560 feet (171 meters) long. They have a displacement of 18,750 tons (17,010 metric tons). The *Ohio*-class subs can reach speeds greater than 25 knots. They carry 24 nuclear missiles.

The Navy has 18 *Ohio*-class subs. Each of these subs carries about 140 enlisted personnel and 15 officers. Officers are college graduates. Enlisted personnel have a great deal of specialized training.

Early Attack Subs

In 1959, the Navy commissioned its first nuclear attack sub. This sub was called the *Skipjack*. The *Skipjack* was 252 feet (77 meters) long and had a displacement of 3,513 tons (3,187 metric tons). *Skipjack* could travel at more than 30 knots. It was the fastest sub in the Navy.

Skipjack was streamlined. The Navy called its design a "tear drop." The sub was shaped like a tear that falls from a person's eye. This streamlined shape helped *Skipjack*-class subs travel faster than previous subs. All U.S. nuclear subs built after the *Skipjack* also have this shape. The Navy commissioned five other *Skipjack*-class subs.

The *Skipjack's* streamlined shape helped it travel faster than previous subs.

The Navy continued to produce new attack subs. It wanted subs that could submerge deeper. In 1961, the Navy commissioned a new class of attack subs. These ships were named after a ship called *Permit.* They were 278 feet (85 meters) long and had a displacement of 4,300 tons (3,901 metric tons). They could dive to more than 800 feet (244 meters). Previous subs could dive only about 700 feet (210 meters) underwater.

In 1967, the Navy commissioned improved versions of *Permit*-class subs. These subs were in the *Sturgeon* class. *Sturgeon*-class subs were 292 feet (89 meters) long and had a displacement of about 4,700 tons (4,260 metric tons).

Today's Attack Subs

Today, *Los Angeles* and *Seawolf*-class subs are the only attack subs in the Navy's active service. In 1976, the Navy commissioned *Los Angeles*-class attack subs. These subs are 360 feet (110 meters) long and have a displacement of more than 6,900 tons (6,260 metric tons). They have a top speed of about 30 knots. The Navy has about 50 *Los Angeles*-class subs. Each sub sails with about 115 enlisted personnel and 12 officers.

In 1997, the Navy commissioned *Seawolf*-class attack subs. These subs are 353 feet (108 meters) long and have a displacement of 9,137 tons (8,289 metric tons). Their top speed is about 35 knots.

Permit-class subs could dive to more than 800 feet (244 meters) underwater.

The Navy commissioned *Seawolf*-class subs in 1997.

The Navy has three *Seawolf*-class subs. Each sub sails with about 120 enlisted personnel and 14 officers. *Seawolf*-class subs are the quietest subs in the Navy.

Nuclear Submarines in Action

Nuclear subs have performed many missions throughout their history. In the mid-1940s, the United States became involved in a struggle with the Soviet Union. This struggle was called the Cold War.

The United States believed in democracy. People can elect their leaders in countries with this form of government. The U.S. government wanted other countries to practice democracy. But the Soviet Union believed in communism. People cannot choose their leaders in countries with this form of government. The Soviet government wanted to spread communism to other countries.

No direct battles occurred between the U.S. and the Soviet Union during the Cold War. But each country feared that the other would try to start a war. The United States and the Soviet Union used their militaries to threaten each other. Each country worked to have superior military vehicles, ships, and weapons.

The Navy's nuclear subs were an important part of the Cold War. The U.S. Navy threatened the Soviet Union by sailing fleet ballistic missile subs in nearby waters. It used attack subs to threaten Soviet ballistic missile subs. The U.S. Navy also used its submarines to gather information about Soviet actions. The Cold War ended in 1991. That year, the Soviet Union was divided into Russia and several smaller countries.

In 1991, the Navy used *Los Angeles*-class subs in the Gulf War (1991). This war started after the Middle Eastern country of Iraq invaded neighboring Kuwait. The United States helped force Iraq's military out of Kuwait. *Los Angeles*-class subs fired Tomahawk cruise missiles at Iraqi targets. Computers guide these missiles to their targets. Tomahawk missiles had direct hits on about 85 percent of their targets during the war.

Los Angeles-class subs often patrol the world's oceans.

During peacetime, nuclear submarines patrol oceans. They remain ready for combat at all times. They travel near countries that are at war with each other. Their actions may help the leaders of warring countries to agree to peace.

Chapter Three

On Board a Nuclear Sub

Nuclear subs have several parts. These parts include the hull, the engine, the control room, and several weapons. Nuclear subs are designed to carry a great deal of equipment and supplies. The subs also have several safety features.

The Hull

The body of a sub is called the hull. The hull must keep out water and resist water pressure. Water pressure is the weight of the water that presses down on a sub. Water pressure increases as subs travel deeper underwater. Most subs have an inner hull called the pressure hull to resist

A sub's control room contains a great deal of equipment to steer the sub and control its depth.

Nuclear Power

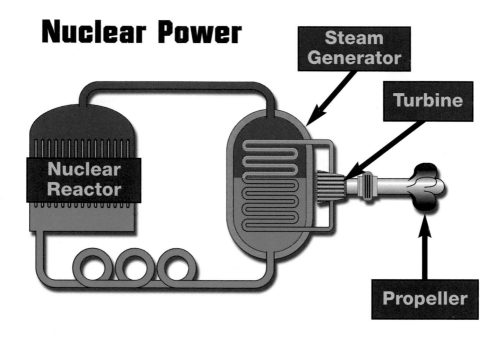

water pressure. The pressure hull is made of thick steel plates bent into a circle.

The hull's front tip is called the bow. This area often holds sonar equipment. Sonar equipment uses sound waves to detect objects underwater. The sonar equipment sends this information to computers. Crewmembers then study the information to see if the sonar has found an enemy sub. Some Navy subs also carry sonar equipment on the sides of the hull. Most subs also use a cable to tow sonar equipment behind them.

The Reactor

A nuclear reactor powers a nuclear sub's engine. It is located near the sub's center. The reactor's center is made of many thin plates that contain uranium. The uranium atoms split to release large amounts of radiation.

The splitting of the atoms starts a process that powers the sub. It first heats water in the nuclear reactor. The water travels to a steam generator. This machine uses the hot water to create a second system of steam. The steam then powers a motor called a turbine. The turbine turns a propeller. This set of rotating blades is located outside the sub at the hull's rear. The propeller moves the sub through the water.

Rudder and Hydroplanes

Some features help a sub travel through the water. A rudder is located at the hull's rear near the propeller. Crewmembers use this piece of metal to steer the sub left or right.

Metal plates called hydroplanes also help crewmembers control a sub. Hydroplanes tilt the sub up or down. They usually are located at the front and back of a sub. Subs also may have hydroplanes on the conning tower. This covered tower is located near the sub's front on top of the hull.

The Control Room

The control room is located below the conning tower. Crewmembers operate the sub from the control room. The control room has a tube-shaped viewing device called a periscope. It allows crewmembers to see the water's surface when the sub is submerged.

The control room has many types of equipment. Navigation computers help crewmembers locate the sub's position

Some subs have hydroplanes on the conning tower.

underwater. Computers also control the sub's weapons. Radar equipment in the control room uses radio waves to detect objects on the water's surface or on land.

Submarines need to add or lose weight inside the hull to control their depth. This weight is called ballast. Subs use water for ballast. The ballast is stored in two sets of tanks. The main

Attack subs may fire Tomahawk cruise missiles.

set is located outside the pressure hull. The other is inside the pressure hull.

The control room has a ballast control panel. Crewmembers use the panel to adjust the amount of ballast. They let air out of the main ballast tanks to sink. The tanks then fill with water. Crewmembers use air to blow water out of the main tanks to rise to the surface. Air then fills the tanks.

Weapons

Attack submarines launch torpedoes from torpedo tubes on their sides. *Los Angeles*-class subs have four torpedo tubes. Subs in the *Seawolf* class have eight tubes. Most attack subs launch MK-48 torpedoes. A wire is attached to these torpedoes. Crewmembers use the wire to guide the torpedo when they fire it. The torpedo then uses sonar to locate its target.

Most attack subs also can fire Tomahawk cruise missiles. Torpedo tubes on the sub's sides launch these missiles. Torpedo tubes on top of the sub's hull also may fire the missiles.

Attack subs lay various types of mines. They may lay CAPTOR mines. These mines can detect ships by sound, magnetism, or water pressure. The mines are attached to a weight on the ocean floor. The mine floats above the weight. The CAPTOR mine releases a torpedo when it detects a ship. Attack subs also may lay the Submarine-Launched Mobile Mine (SLMM).

This mine lies at the bottom of the ocean. It explodes when a ship passes above it.

Fleet ballistic missile subs carry Trident missiles. These missiles are launched from large vertical tubes in the middle of the sub. The missiles then travel in a straight line toward the target. Trident missiles can travel more than 20,000 feet (6,096 meters) per second. Fleet ballistic missile subs also carry MK-48 torpedoes.

Crewmembers

Navy crewmembers choose to work on subs. These volunteers first receive basic submarine training. They then take classes in one subject. For example, a crewmember may learn how to operate sonar equipment or repair nuclear reactors.

Crewmembers usually work for six hours at a time. In their spare time, they may study to learn new skills. They also may perform drills. These practice sessions help them learn what to do during an emergency.

Sub tenders carry food and supplies to submarines.

Crewmembers sleep on small beds called bunks. Three bunks usually are stacked on top of each other against a wall. Crewmembers sometimes share a bunk. This practice is called "hot bunking." It allows one crewmember to sleep while another works.

A fleet ballistic missile sub has missile tubes on its top.

Support and Supplies

The Navy has ships called sub tenders. These ships provide food and supplies to subs. The tenders also carry missiles and torpedoes to replace weapons a sub has used during battle. The tenders may deliver mail to the sub's crewmembers.

Sub tenders also carry specially trained crewmembers. Some of these personnel are trained to maintain subs. Doctors and dentists are aboard tenders in case sub crewmembers need medical or dental attention.

Safety

A nuclear sub has features that help keep the sub and its crewmembers safe. One of these features is an escape hatch. Crewmembers can leave the sub through this doorway to small rescue subs during emergencies.

Crewmembers also can leave a sub wearing a Steinke hood. This hood fits over a crewmember's head and chest. It has a supply of air for the crewmember to breathe. But a Steinke hood cannot be used at depths of more than 400 feet (122 meters). The hood cannot support the water pressure at this depth.

A sub may need to reach the surface quickly during an emergency. The ballast control panel has an emergency system to release a great deal of ballast. This system can work even if a sub loses power.

A nuclear sub's crew is trained to operate the nuclear reactor. Small amounts of radiation are

not very harmful to people. But large amounts of it can kill people. Crewmembers make sure most of the radiation stays inside the reactor. The reactor also is placed behind specially constructed thick walls called bulkheads. The walls shield other areas of the sub from radiation.

Subs also have equipment that keeps the air safe to breathe. People release a gas called carbon dioxide when they breathe out. People can die if they breathe in too much carbon dioxide. Equipment on a sub removes carbon dioxide from the air.

Subs have other equipment that provides safe water. People cannot safely drink ocean water because it contains a great deal of salt. Subs have a water distiller that removes the salt. Crewmembers use this fresh water for drinking, cooking, and washing. The reactor and the steam plant also need fresh water. A nuclear sub's water distiller can provide about 10,000 gallons (37,850 liters) of fresh water each day.

A sub's equipment helps its crewmembers live comfortably.

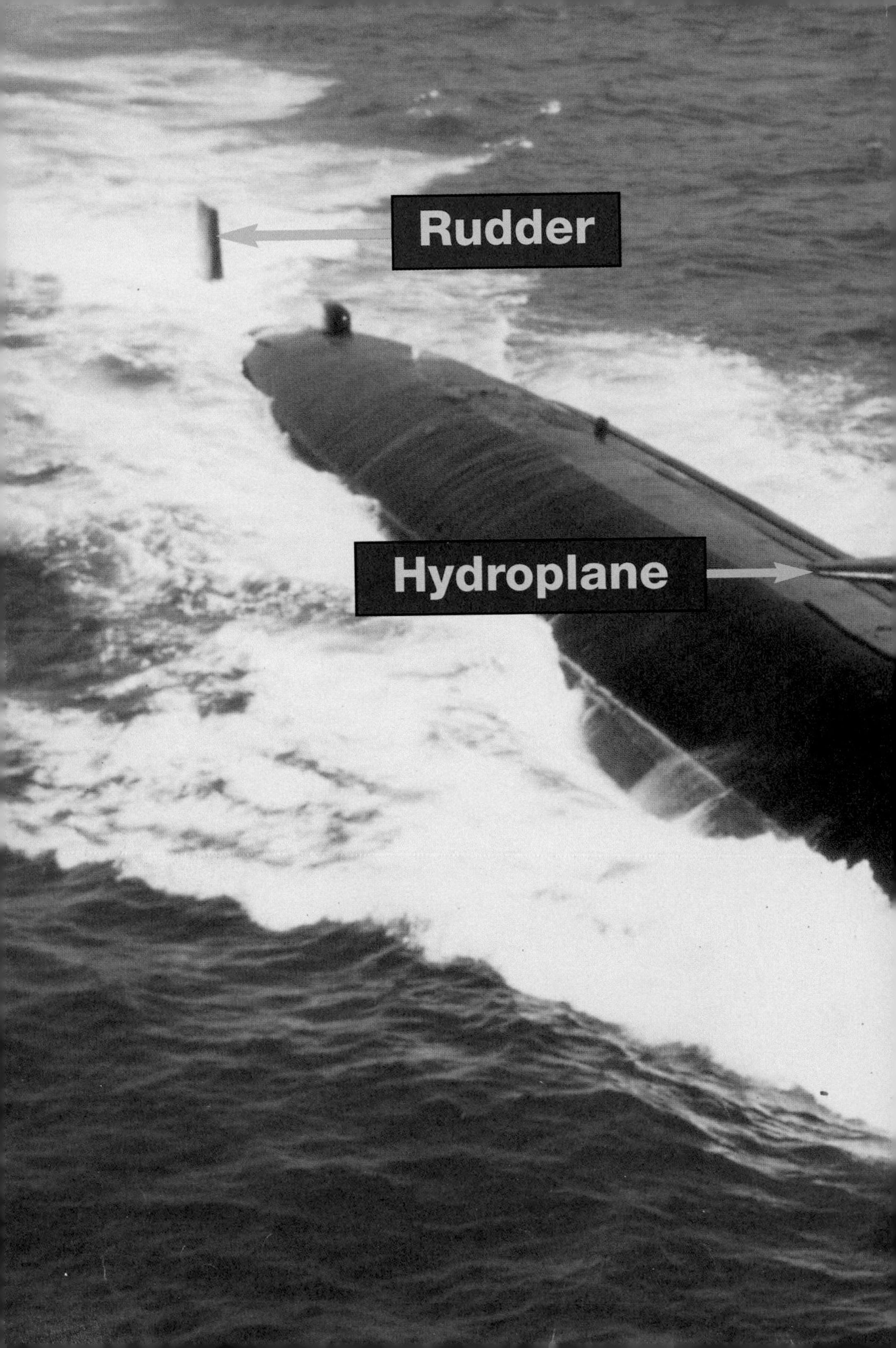

Rudder

Hydroplane

Hydroplane

Conning Tower

Hull

Chapter Four

Nuclear Sub Missions

Nuclear submarines perform a variety of missions. They support other warships. They have equipment to help crewmembers watch and report enemy movements.

Types of Missions

Most of the Navy's subs are attack subs. These subs are equipped for ASW missions. But they also can perform other missions. Attack subs patrol with other warships to help defend the ships from enemy attacks. Attack subs also perform surveillance missions. The subs patrol near enemy ports or ships to gather information.

Attack subs also take part in sea denial missions. Subs stay hidden near an enemy port to

Nuclear subs sometimes perform missions in ice-covered waters.

prevent enemy ships from leaving the area. The enemy usually chooses to keep its ships in port instead of risking an attack by the sub. Subs must remain submerged for long periods of time during sea denial missions.

Fleet ballistic missile subs are usually on patrol. Their main purpose is to threaten enemies' important resources so that they will not attack the United States. For example, crewmembers may fire missiles at an enemy's factories, bridges, or railroads during an attack.

Special Operations

Each branch of the military has a Special Operations Force. Members of these forces assist the military with dangerous secret missions.

Members of the Navy's Special Operation Force are called SEALs. SEALs are trained for sea, air, and land combat. Some attack subs are specially designed to transport SEALs. Two redesigned fleet ballistic missile subs also transport SEALs. These transport subs have a Dry Deck Shelter (DDS) on top of the hull to

Attack subs may perform ASW, sea denial, or surveillance missions.

hold a Swimmer Delivery Vehicle (SDV). Small groups of SEALs can travel in these tiny subs.

Virginia-Class Subs

The Navy is currently designing *Virginia*-class subs. The Navy plans to commission these new nuclear attack subs in 2004. *Virginia*-class subs will be 377 feet (115 meters) long and have a displacement of 7,700 tons (6,985 metric tons). These subs will carry torpedoes and missiles.

They also will launch small subs that do not carry crewmembers. The Navy will use these computer-controlled subs to gather enemy information.

Virginia-class subs will be the first subs without a periscope. Instead, these subs will have a video camera system for crewmembers to view their surroundings.

The military is designing *Virginia*-class subs to perform a variety of missions. The subs will do surveillance and minelaying missions. They will launch missiles to attack land targets. *Virginia*-class subs also will perform search-and-rescue missions and protect other warships from attacks.

The Navy plans to produce about 30 *Virginia*-class subs. In the future, the Navy may design more new sub classes to perform submarine missions.

Nuclear subs will continue to perform important missions in the future.

Words to Know

conning tower (KON-ing TOU-ur)—a covered tower on top of many submarine hulls

hatch (HACH)—a doorway of a submarine

hull (HUHL)—the body of a submarine

hydroplane (HYE-druh-plane)—a movable metal plate that tilts a submarine up or down

periscope (PER-uh-skope)—a tube-shaped viewing device; crewmembers can use a periscope to view the water's surface from a submerged submarine.

reactor (ree-AK-tur)—a large machine in which nuclear energy is produced by splitting atoms under controlled conditions

rudder (RUHD-ur)—a movable metal plate that steers a submarine left or right

sonar (SOH-nar)—a device that uses sound waves to locate underwater objects

turbine (TUR-buhn)—an engine powered by steam, water, or gas

To Learn More

Davies, Roy. *Nautilus: The Story of Man Under the Sea.* Annapolis, Md.: Naval Institute Press, 1995.

Genat, Robert, and Robin Genat. *Modern United States Navy Submarines.* Enthusiast Color Series. Osceola, Wis.: Motorbooks International, 1997.

Green, Michael. *Submarines.* Land and Sea. Mankato, Minn.: Capstone High-Interest Books, 1998.

Tall, Jeff. *The History of Submarines.* The History of. Hauppauge, N.Y.: Barron's Educational Series, 1998.

Useful Addresses

Chief of Naval Operations
Submarine Warfare Division (N87)
2000 Navy Pentagon
Washington, DC 20350-2600

**Historic Ship *Nautilus* and Submarine
 Force Museum**
Naval Submarine Base, New London
Groton, CT 06349-5571

Naval Historical Center
Washington Navy Yard
805 Kidder Breese SE
Washington, DC 20374-5060

United States Naval Submarine School
Box 700, Code 01B
Groton, CT 06349-5700

Internet Sites

Attack Submarines
http://www.chinfo.navy.mil/navpalib/factfile/
　ships/ship-ssn.html

Fleet Ballistic Missile Submarines
http://www.chinfo.navy.mil/navpalib/factfile/
　ships/ship-ssbn.html

Undersea Warfare Magazine
http://www.chinfo.navy.mil/navpalib/cno/n87/
　usw.html

United States Navy
http://www.navy.mil

Index

ASW, 7

ballast, 27, 28, 33
bow, 24

Cold War, 19, 20
communism, 19
computers, 20, 24, 26–27
conning tower, 26
control room, 23, 26–27, 28

democracy, 19

engine, 6, 11, 23, 25

hatch, 33
hull, 23–24, 25, 26, 27, 28,
    29, 40
hydroplanes, 26

knot, 11, 14, 16

mine, 9, 29–30
missile, 5, 9, 13, 14, 20,
    29–30, 32, 40, 43

officers, 14, 16, 18

periscope, 26, 43
propeller, 25, 26

radiation, 25, 33, 35
reactor, 25, 30, 33, 35
Rickover, Hyman, 11
rudder, 26

SDV, 41
SLMM, 29
sonar, 24, 29
Soviet Union, 19, 20
Steinke hood, 33

torpedo, 9, 29, 30,
    32, 41
turbine, 25

uranium, 6, 25

water pressure, 23–24,
    29, 33